Smoothies For Weight Loss

Table of Contents

Introduction 5

Why Are Smoothies Good for Your Health?.....................6

Detox Your Body...7

Glow From The Inside, Lose Weight & Improve Your Health 8

Bonus Tips...9

   Breakfast Sweet Smoothies 9

   Lunch Smoothies 10

   Dinner Green Smoothies 11

1. Sweet Smoothies 12

   Vanilla-Berry Blast..12

   Pumpkin & Fig Smoothie 14

   Minty Grapefruit with Lime..16

   Orange Antioxidant Refresher..18

   Cranberry Beet 20

   Sweet Sumo Kiwi 22

   Pumpkin Powerhouse Smoothie 24

   Sage Blackberry 26

   Turmeric Ginger Smoothie 28

   Mini Pepper Popper Smoothie..30

   Strawberry Lime Smoothie 32

   Fresh Purple Fig Smoothie..34

   Strawberry Beet Smoothie 36

   Blueberry Crumble Smoothie..38

Chia-Berry Belly Blaster...40

Peppermint Stick Smoothie 42

Carrot Coconut Smoothie..44

Persimmon Mango 46

Persimmon Pineapple Protein Smoothie.....................48

Ginger Detox Smoothie 50

2. Nutritional Smoothies...52

Sapodilla, Chia, And Almond Milk Smoothie 52

Apple, Dried Figs, And Lemon Smoothie 54

Orange, Lemon, And Flax Seeds Smoothie...................56

Celery, Pear, And ACV Smoothie 58

Carrot, Watermelon, And Cumin Smoothie 60

Tomato, Grape, And Lime Smoothie 62

Grapefruit, Pineapple, And Black Pepper Smoothie 64

Blueberry, Oats, And Chia Smoothie 66

Cucumber, Plum, And Cumin Smoothie 68

Peach, Passion Fruit, And Flax Seeds Smoothie..............70

Green Apple, Lettuce, And Honey Smoothie 72

Strawberry, Black Grape, And Ginger Smoothie 74

Kiwi, Apricot, And Cantaloupe Smoothie 76

Raspberry, Chia, And Coconut Water Smoothie 78

Gourd, Cucumber, And Lemon Smoothie 80

Beetroot, Black Grape, And Mint Smoothie 82

Spinach, Strawberry, And Cinnamon Smoothie.............84

Banana, Almond, And Dark Chocolate Smoothie 86

Papaya, Lemon, And Cayenne Pepper Smoothie 88

Pomegranate, Tangerine, And Ginger Smoothie.............90

3. Green Smoothies 92

Cucumber Ginger Green Smoothie 92

Peach Green Smoothie 94

Peach Walnut Smoothie 96

Fat-Burning Green Smoothie...............................98

Cucumber-Mint Smoothie...................................100

Mango Matcha Green Smoothie...........................102

Green Spirulina Smoothie 104

Cold Buster Citrus Green Smoothie 106

Creamy Kiwi Smoothie.......................................108

Chia Seed Smoothie 110

Green Monster Smoothie 112

Spicy Tropical Greens Delight.............................114

Strawberry Spinach Green Smoothie....................116

Vanilla-Mint Green Smoothie..............................118

Tropical Green Smoothie....................................120

Basil Cantaloupe Smoothie.................................122

Banana Blueberry Gooseberry Green Smoothie 124

Kale Skin Tonic Green Smoothie.........................126

Coconut Oil Detox Green Smoothie 128

Broccoli Detox Smoothie 130

Main Ingredients Used and its Benefits.................132

Conclusion 137

Introduction

Thank you for downloading the book "60 Delicious refreshing smoothies Recipes for Weight Loss." If you're getting tired of changing one diet plan to another for losing your belly fat, so there is no need to worry.

Summer is right around the corner, and that means swimsuit and beach season is almost here. It also means that a lot of people want to lose weight quickly and keep it off long term. Now you have a fast and effective fat burning solution that will allow you to lose weight in a healthy way so that you don't look sick and washed out.

This books gives you the best way to lose your belly fat by adding delicious smoothies to your daily routine.

Why Are Smoothies Good for Your Health?

Smoothies are full of fiber, vitamins, and nutrients. Smoothies are very helpful for improving your digestive system, immune system, maintain your blood sugar, cholesterol level, blood flow, and definitely for weight loss. All the smoothies in this book also give you enough energy, which is necessary for your body.

Smoothie Cleanses are all the rage right now. Nutribullets and blenders are selling like hot cakes, and it is common to see people walking down the street sipping on brightly colored drinks. Well, now you can join them and take the first step to achieving extraordinary health!

Ingredients required for making these smoothies are easily available in your nearby market. Smoothies in this book are very easy to prepare. It requires hardly 5-6 minutes to make your yummy smoothies. Trust me you can shed pounds simply by drinking these smoothies.

So here we start the journey to weight loss!

Detox Your Body

This detox is all about healing and repairing your body from the inside out, using REAL food by consuming pure raw nutrition. It's so easy that virtually anyone can follow this super simple and effortless plan. After the detox, you are guaranteed to feel more confident and look better in clothes. In fact, there is a chance you may have to splash out on a new wardrobe as you will not be able to fit into the clothes you are wearing today!

Health benefits during and after the detox:

- Release the toxins from your body that make it hard to lose weight and keep it off
- Better digestion
- Rapid weight loss by putting your body into 'Fat Burning Mode'
- Reprogram your brain to stop cravings
- Nourish your cells from the inside out
- Gain sustained energy throughout the day

Glow From The Inside, Lose Weight & Improve Your Health

The most common form of weight loss is to exercise vigorously and drastically reduce the number of calories in your diet. This has been proven to be one of the worst ways to lose weight, and it is also guaranteed that the dieter will regain all of the weight they worked so hard to lose.

The reason this method is unsuccessful is because your body enters starvation mode, and your hormones come into action in order to fight against the weight your body is losing and holds onto body fat. If you can relate to this and have struggled to keep the weight off while dieting, then it is likely your hormones have been the reason you were unable to achieve your goal weight.

Bonus Tips

Breakfast Sweet Smoothies

A nutritious breakfast smoothie gives a good start to your day. It gives you the energy to keep going all day long. In the summer, people around the world look for ways to blend flavor and good nutrition together and get relief from the scorching heat. Having smoothies with breakfast every day can surely pave the way for good health and enjoyment throughout the hot season.

It also prevents dehydration: Water is the most abundant thing both on earth and in your body. About 70 percent of your body is water. Having breakfast smoothies is a great way to replenish the loss of water in your body during the summer.

Detoxifies your body
Foods like garlic, papaya, and beets help cleanse your blood and get rid of several toxins accumulated in your body tissues. Thus, to have a great breakfast you should include smoothies as reliable detoxifying drinks every day.

Keeps Blood Sugar in Check
High blood sugar and diabetes are the most common lifestyle diseases that bother people all around the world. People who have imbalanced sugar levels in their blood are prone to

several complications. Thus having a breakfast that is rich in nutrients but low in calories can make things easier.

Lunch Smoothies

Makes you feel full: People trying to lose weight often skip the morning meal and end up snacking on food in larger amounts between meals. To avoid this, experts advise having smoothies made of excellent fruits and flavors so that you stay full for a long time.

Controls Cravings

Smoothies are full of nutrients and flavor. They are an essential part of the best luches, as they provide a power-packed start for the day. A lot of protein along with many nutrients subdue food cravings and keep you away from eating junk food.

Boosts Brain Power

It is quite evident that certain fruits and vegetables increase brain power and boost memory. Mental alertness and concentration is greatly enhanced by ingredients like coconut that are rich in omega-3 fatty acids. Smoothies with these ingredients help the brain work faster.

Dinner Green Smoothies

Health and nutrition experts worldwide suggest consuming liquid food for better digestion. Smoothies contain blended fruits and vegetables in liquid form that make it easier for the body to break them down.

Curbs Better Digestion

People belonging to different age groups around the world often face issues related to lack of sleep and restlessness. A healthy dinner accompanied by a smoothie made of bananas, kiwi, and oats provides calcium and magnesium in good amounts. This induces sleep and helps maintain healthy sleeping patterns.

Aid in Digestion

Green smoothies that contain a lot of green leafy vegetables add essential vitamins and minerals to dinner and aid in digestion. The fiber supplied by these drinks multiplies the benefits of having a delicious dinner smoothie, especially during the summer.

Provides a Good Amount of Fiber

The most common problem people suffer from today is related to upset bowels. A good amount of fibrous food is essential for regulating the excretory system so that you can enjoy summer without worrying about your health. Smoothies with a lot of fruits and vegetables help keep your bowels functioning smoothly.

1. Sweet Smoothies

Vanilla-Berry Blast

Calories: 148/**Fat:** 5g

Carbohydrates: 26g /**Protein:** 4g

Prep Time: 5 minutes

Servings: 2

Ingredients

- 1 quart plain nonfat Greek yogurt
- 8 oz. unsweetened frozen strawberries or blueberries
- 2 cup unsweetened vanilla almond milk

- 1 banana, frozen
- 1 tsp. cinnamon

Instructions

1. Add half of the yogurt, berries, and milk into a blender and blend until smooth.
2. Add the remainder of the ingredients and blend until smooth.

Pumpkin & Fig Smoothie

Calories: 211/**Fat:** 5g

Carbohydrates: 18g/**Protein:** 12g

Prep Time: 10 minutes

Servings: 2

Ingredients

- 1/2 large frozen banana
- 3 fresh figs, peeled and chopped
- 1/3 cup canned pumpkin
- 2 tbsp. cinnamon almond butter
- 1 cup milk
- 2-3 ice cubes

14

- 1 tbsp. hemp seeds
- cinnamon to garnish

Instructions

1. Add banana, figs, pumpkin, almond butter, milk, and ice to a blender and blend on high until very smooth.
2. Pour into a glass, then top with the hemp hearts and a shake of cinnamon. Serve immediately.

Minty Grapefruit with Lime

Calories: 187/**Fat:** 7g

Carbohydrates: 30g/**Protein:** 5g

Prep Time: 5 minutes

Servings: 2

Ingredients

- 1 grapefruit, peeled
- 1 banana, peeled
- ½ lime, juiced
- 3 sprigs mint
- ½ tsp. maqui berry powder
- 3 tbsp. Walnuts

- 1 cup water
- 1 cup ice

Instructions

1. Place all ingredients into a blender and blend until smooth, creamy, and no chunks remain.
2. Serve and enjoy immediately or store in the fridge for up to 24 hours.

Orange Antioxidant Refresher

Calories: 101/**Fat:** 1g

Carbohydrates: 25g/**Protein:** 2g

Prep Time: 5 minutes

Servings: 2

Ingredients

- 4 oz. pineapple
- 1 mini orange cauliflower, leaves removed
- 1 orange, peeled
- 1/2 tsp. turmeric
- 1/2 tsp. ginger
- 1 tsp. pomegranate powder

- 1 cup water
- 1 cup ice

Instructions

1. Place all ingredients into a blender and blend until smooth, creamy, and no chunks remain.
2. Serve and enjoy immediately or store in the fridge for up to 24 hours.

Cranberry Beet

Calories: 150/**Fat:** 7g

Carbohydrates: 18g/**Protein:** 5g

Prep Time: 5 minutes

Servings: 2

Ingredients

- 1 1/2 oz. baby kale
- 4 oz beets, scrubbed and chopped
- 3 oz. cranberries
- 1 tangerine, peeled
- 1/2 inch ginger
- 1 tsp. pomegranate powder

- 3 tbsp. walnuts
- 1 cup water
- 1 cup ice

Instructions

1. Place all ingredients into a blender and blend until smooth, creamy, and no chunks remain.
2. Serve and enjoy immediately or store in the fridge for up to 24 hours.

Sweet Sumo Kiwi

Calories: 148/**Fat:** 5g

Carbohydrates: 26g/**Protein:** 4g

Prep Time: 5 minutes

Servings: 2

Ingredients

- 1 orange, peeled
- 1 kiwi, peeled
- 4 oz. pineapple
- 1 tsp. mangosteen
- 3 tbsp. Almonds

- 1 cup water
- 1 cup ice

Instructions

1. Place all ingredients into a blender.
2. Blend until smooth and no chunks remain.
3. Serve and enjoy.

Pumpkin Powerhouse Smoothie

Calories: 148/**Fat:** 5g

Carbohydrates: 26g/**Protein:** 4g

Prep Time: 5 minutes

Servings: 2

Ingredients

- 1 cup pumpkin puree, canned or fresh

- 1 cup unsweetened vanilla almond milk

- 1/2 frozen banana

- handful of ice cubes

- dash of pumpkin pie spice (swap for cinnamon if you don't have this)

Instructions

1. Blend all ingredients together and enjoy.

Sage Blackberry

Calories: 154/**Fat:** 6g

Carbohydrates: 24g /**Protein:** 3g

Prep Time: 5 minutes

Servings: 2

Ingredients

- 1 oz. blackberries
- 4 oz. pineapple
- 1 pear, chopped
- 3 sage leaves
- 1/2 tsp. maqui berry powder (easily available on amazon)
- 3 tbsp. cashews

- 1 cup water
- 1 cup ice

Instructions

1. Place all ingredients into a blender and blend until smooth, creamy, and no chunks remain.
2. Serve and enjoy immediately or store in the fridge for up to 24 hours.

Turmeric Ginger Smoothie

Calories: 86/**Fat:** 3g

Carbohydrates: 4g /**Protein:** 3g

Prep Time: 5 minutes

Servings: 2

Ingredients

- 1 yellow squash, chopped
- 1 orange, peeled
- 1 oz. kumquats
- 1 inch turmeric, chopped
- 1/2 inch ginger, peeled, chopped
- 1 tbsp. hemp seeds

- 1 cup water
- 1 cup ice

Instructions

1. Place all ingredients into a blender and blend until smooth
2. Serve and enjoy immediately.

Mini Pepper Popper Smoothie

Calories: 190/**Fat:** 8g

Carbohydrates: 21g/**Protein:** 5g

Prep Time: 5 minutes

Servings: 2

Ingredients

- 5 oz. mini peppers, seeded
- 1 orange, peeled
- 4 oz. pineapple
- 1/2 lemon, juiced
- 1 tsp. rose hips powder

- 3 tbsp. almonds
- 1 cup water
- 1 cup ice

Instructions

1. Place all ingredients into a blender and blend until smooth, creamy, and no chunks remain.
2. Serve and enjoy immediately or store in the fridge for up to 24 hours.

Strawberry Lime Smoothie

Calories: 130/**Fat:** 2g

Carbohydrates: 25g/**Protein:** 3g

Prep Time: 5 minutes

Servings: 2

Ingredients

- 1 1/2 oz. baby spinach
- 1 banana, peeled
- 3 oz. strawberries
- 1/2 lime, juiced
- 1 tbsp. flaxseed
- 1 tsp. baobab powder

- 1 cup coconut water
- 1 cup ice

Instructions

1. Place all ingredients into a blender and blend until smooth, creamy, and no chunks remain.
2. Serve and enjoy immediately or store in the fridge for up to 24 hours.

Fresh Purple Fig Smoothie

Calories: 136/**Fat:** 4g

Carbohydrates: 28g/**Protein:** 3g

Prep Time: 5 minutes

Servings: 2

Ingredients

- 1 fig
- 1 cup grapes
- 1 pear, chopped
- 1/2 tsp. maqui powder
- 1 tbsp. hemp seed

- 1 cup water
- 1 cup ice

Instructions

1. Place all ingredients into a blender and blend until smooth, creamy, and no chunks remain.
2. Serve and enjoy immediately or store in the fridge for up to 24 hours.

Strawberry Beet Smoothie

Calories: 128/**Fat:** 2g

Carbohydrates: 26g/**Protein:** 4g

Prep Time: 5 minutes

Servings: 2

Ingredients

- 4 oz. Beets, scrubbed and chopped
- ¼ lbs. strawberries
- 1 orange, peeled
- 1 lemon, juiced
- ½ inch ginger
- 1 tbsp. chia seeds

- 1 cup water
- 1 cup ice

Instructions

1. Place all ingredients into a blender and blend until smooth, creamy, and no chunks remain.
2. Serve and enjoy immediately or store in the fridge for up to 24 hours.

Blueberry Crumble Smoothie

Calories: 128/**Fat:** 8g

Carbohydrates: 14g/**Protein:** 4g

Prep Time: 5 minutes

Servings: 2

Ingredients

- 1 apple, chopped
- 1 oz. blueberries
- 1 yellow squash, chopped
- 1 tsp. acai berry powder
- 3 tbsp. Walnuts

- 1 cup water
- 1 cup ice

Instructions

1. Place all ingredients into a blender and blend until smooth, creamy, and no chunks remain.
2. Serve and enjoy immediately or store in the fridge for up to 24 hours.

Chia-Berry Belly Blaster

Calories: 148/**Fat:** 5g

Carbohydrates: 26g/**Protein:** 4g

Prep Time: 5 minutes

Servings: 2

Ingredients

- 1 cup plain Greek yogurt, unsweetened

- 1 cup frozen berries (blueberries, strawberries, or açai berries make great options)

- 1 tbsp. vanilla extract

- 1 tbsp. ground chia seeds

- 1/2 cup ice

Instructions

1. Blend all ingredients together and enjoy.

Peppermint Stick Smoothie

Calories: 150/**Fat:** 5g

Carbohydrates: 29g /**Protein:** 2g

Prep Time: 5 minutes

Servings: 2

Ingredients

- 1 apple, chopped
- 1 banana, peeled
- 1 tbsp. coconut milk
- 4 sprigs mint
- 1 1/2 tbsp. cacao powder

- 1 cup water
- 1 cup ice

Instructions

1. Place all ingredients into a blender and blend until smooth, creamy, and no chunks remain.
2. Serve and enjoy immediately or store in the fridge for up to 24 hours.

Carrot Coconut Smoothie

Calories: 140/**Fat:** 2g

Carbohydrates: 29g/**Protein:** 2g

Prep Time: 5 minutes

Servings: 2

Ingredients

- 6 oz. carrots, chopped
- 4 oz. pineapple
- 1 orange, peeled
- 2 tbsp. coconut flakes
- 1 tsp. camu camu

- 1 cup water
- 1 cup ice

Instructions

1. Place all ingredients into a blender and blend until smooth, creamy, and no chunks remain.
2. Serve and enjoy immediately or store in the fridge for up to 24 hours.

Persimmon Mango

Calories: 145/**Fat:** 7g

Carbohydrates: 21g/**Protein:** 4g

Prep Time: 5 minutes

Servings: 2

Ingredients

- 1 persimmon, topped
- 1 slice cantaloupe
- 4 oz. mango
- 3 tbsp. walnuts
- 1/2 tsp. camu camu

- 1 cup water
- 1 cup ice

Instructions

1. Place all ingredients into a blender.
2. Blend until smooth and no chunks remain.
3. Serve and enjoy.

Persimmon Pineapple Protein Smoothie

Calories: 159/**Fat:** 2g

Carbohydrates: 33g/**Protein:** 7g

Prep Time: 5 minutes

Servings: 2

Ingredients

- 1 squash
- 1 persimmon, topped and chopped
- 4 oz. pineapple
- 1 tsp. cinnamon
- 1 tbsp. flaxseed

- 1 tbsp. pea protein
- 1 cup water
- 1 cup ice

Instructions

1. Place all ingredients into a blender and blend until smooth, creamy, and no chunks remain.
2. Serve and enjoy immediately or store in the fridge for up to 24 hours.

Ginger Detox Smoothie

Calories: 114/**Fat:** 1g

Carbohydrates: 22g/**Protein:** 5g

Prep Time: 5 minutes

Servings: 2

Ingredients

- 1 1/2 oz. collard greens
- 2 persian cucumbers, chopped
- 1 apple, chopped
- 1 meyer lemon, peeled
- 1/2 inch ginger
- 1/2 tsp. chlorella

- 1 cup water
- 1 cup ice

Instructions

1. Place all ingredients into a blender and blend until smooth, creamy, and no chunks remain.
2. Serve and enjoy immediately or store in the fridge for up to 24 hours.

2. Nutritional Smoothies

Sapodilla, Chia, And Almond Milk Smoothie

Calories: 114/**Fat:** 1g

Carbohydrates: 22g/**Protein:** 5g

Prep Time: 5 minutes

Servings: 2

Ingredients

- 4 medium sapodillas (chikoo or nispero)
- 3 tbsp. chia seeds

- ⅔ cup almond milk
- 1 tbsp. flakes

Instructions

1. Wash the sapodillas. Peel, seed, and roughly chop them.
2. Toss the chopped sapodillas into the blender and add almond milk.
3. Blend into a smooth paste and pour it into two glasses.
4. Add the chia seeds and stir well. Top it with almond flakes before drinking.

Apple, Dried Figs, And Lemon Smoothie

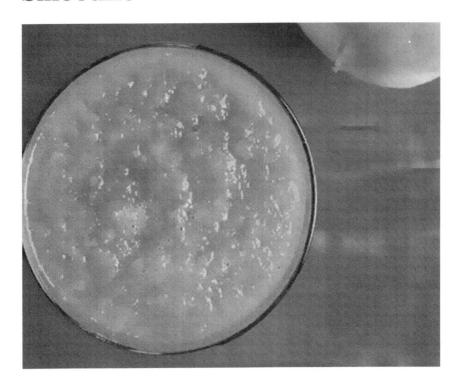

Calories: 120/**Fat:** 2g

Carbohydrates: 25g/**Protein:** 5g

Prep Time: 5 minutes

Servings: 2

Ingredients

- 2 medium apples
- 1 dried fig

54

- ¼ lemon
- a pinch of Himalayan pink salt

Instructions

1. Wash the apples, take the pit out, and roughly chop them.
2. Chop the dried fig.
3. Toss both the chopped apples and figs into a blender.
4. Add lemon juice and give it a stir.
5. Pour the smoothie out into two glasses.
6. Add a pinch of Himalayan pink salt and stir well.

Orange, Lemon, And Flax Seeds Smoothie

Calories: 130/**Fat:** 4g

Carbohydrates: 18g/**Protein:** 3g

Prep Time: 5 minutes

Servings: 2

Ingredients

- 2 large oranges
- 2 tbsp. lemon juice
- 1 tbsp. ground flax seeds
- a pinch of Himalayan pink salt

Instructions

1. Peel the oranges, take out the seeds, and roughly chop them.

2. Toss the chopped oranges into a blender, add lemon juice, and ground the flax seeds.

3. Blend it well and pour out the smoothie into a glass.

4. Add a pinch of Himalayan pink salt and stir well before drinking.

Celery, Pear, And ACV Smoothie

Calories: 114/**Fat:** 1g

Carbohydrates: 22g/**Protein:** 5g

Prep Time: 5 minutes

Servings: 2

Ingredients

- 1 cup chopped celery
- 1 cup chopped pear
- 1 tsp. ACV (apple cider vinegar)
- a pinch of Himalayan pink salt

58

Instructions

1. Toss the chopped celery and pear into a blender.

2. Add a teaspoon of ACV and a pinch of Himalayan pink salt.

3. Stir well before drinking.

Carrot, Watermelon, And Cumin Smoothie

Calories: 114/**Fat:** 1g

Carbohydrates: 22g/**Protein:** 5g

Prep Time: 5 minutes

Servings: 2

Ingredients

- ½ cup chopped carrot
- 1 cup seeded watermelon
- ½ tsp. cumin powder
- a pinch of Himalayan pink salt

Instructions

1. Blend the carrot and watermelon using a bender.

2. Pour the smoothie into a glass.

3. Add cumin powder and a pinch of Himalayan pink salt.

4. Stir well before drinking.

Tomato, Grape, And Lime Smoothie

Calories: 116/**Fat:** 2g

Carbohydrates: 21g/**Protein:** 5g

Prep Time: 5 minutes

Servings: 2

Ingredients

- 2 medium tomatoes
- ½ cup green grapes

- 2 tbsp. lime juice
- a pinch of Himalayan pink salt

Instructions

1. Wash and chop the tomatoes.
2. Toss them into a blender.
3. Add the grapes to the blender and give it a spin.
4. Pour the smoothie into two glasses.
5. Add a tablespoon of lime juice to each glass.
6. Add a pinch of Himalayan pink salt and stir well.

Grapefruit, Pineapple, And Black Pepper Smoothie

Calories: 121/**Fat:** 1g

Carbohydrates: 15g/**Protein:** 3g

Prep Time: 5 minutes

Servings: 2

Ingredients

- 1 cup chopped grapefruit
- 1 cup ripe pineapple
- ½ tsp. freshly ground black pepper
- a pinch of Himalayan pink salt

Instructions

1. Toss the grapefruit and pineapple into a blender and give it a spin.

2. Pour the smoothie out into two glasses.

3. Add black pepper and a pinch of Himalayan pink salt and stir well.

Blueberry, Oats, And Chia Smoothie

Calories: 140/**Fat:** 3g

Carbohydrates: 25g /**Protein:** 6g

Prep Time: 5 minutes

Servings: 2

Ingredients

- ½ cup blueberries
- ¼ cup oats

- 2 tbsp. chia seeds
- 2 cups low-fat milk

Instructions

1. Blend the blueberries, oats, chia seeds, and milk.
2. Pour the smoothie out into two glasses and enjoy!

Cucumber, Plum, And Cumin Smoothie

Calories: 115/**Fat:** 3g

Carbohydrates: 15g/**Protein:** 5g

Prep Time: 5 minutes

Servings: 2

Ingredients

- 2 cups cucumber
- ½ cup plum
- 1 tsp. cumin powder
- 1 tbsp. lime juice
- a pinch of Himalayan pink salt

Instructions

1. Toss the cucumber and plum into a blender and give it a spin.

2. Pour the smoothie out into two glasses and add cumin powder, lime juice, and a pinch of Himalayan pink salt.

3. Stir well before drinking.

Peach, Passion Fruit, And Flax Seeds Smoothie

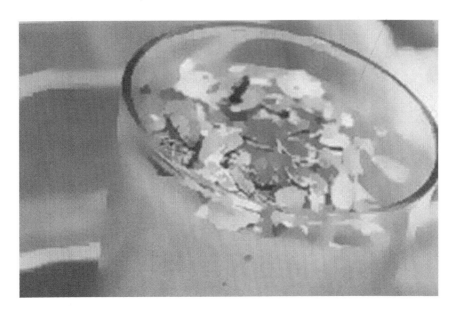

Calories: 114/**Fat:** 1g

Carbohydrates: 22g/**Protein:** 5g

Prep Time: 5 minutes

Servings: 2

Ingredients

- 2 peaches, chopped
- ½ cup passion fruit
- 1 tbsp. ground flax seeds
- a pinch of Himalayan pink salt

Instructions

1. Blend the chopped peach and passion fruit.

2. Pour the smoothie into a glass, add the ground flax seeds, and a pinch of Himalayan pink salt.

3. Stir well before drinking.

Green Apple, Lettuce, And Honey Smoothie

Calories: 114/**Fat:** 6g

Carbohydrates: 21g/**Protein:** 3g

Prep Time: 5 minutes

Servings: 2

Ingredients

- 2 cup chopped green apple
- 1 cup chopped iceberg lettuce
- ½ cup chilled water
- 2 tbsp. organic honey
- a pinch of Himalayan pink salt

Instructions

1. Toss the apple and lettuce into a blender and give it a spin.
2. Add chilled water and stir well before pouring it into two glasses.
3. Add honey and a pinch of Himalayan pink salt.
4. Stir well before drinking.

Strawberry, Black Grape, And Ginger Smoothie

Calories: 114/**Fat:** 1g

Carbohydrates: 22g/**Protein:** 5g

Prep Time: 5 minutes

Servings: 2

Ingredients

- ½ cup strawberries
- 1 cup black grape
- 1 inch crushed ginger root
- 1 tsp. cumin powder
- a pinch of black salt

Instructions

1. Blend the strawberries, black grape, and ginger.

2. Pour the smoothie into two glasses and add cumin powder and Himalayan pink salt.

3. Stir well and drink.

Kiwi, Apricot, And Cantaloupe Smoothie

Calories: 120/**Fat:** 6g

Carbohydrates: 20g/**Protein:** 4g

Prep Time: 5 minutes

Servings: 2

Ingredients

- ½ cup kiwi
- 2 dried apricots, chopped
- 1 cup cantaloupe
- ¼ cup chilled water

76

- 2 tbsp. lime juice
- a pinch of Himalayan pink salt

Instructions

1. Toss the kiwi, apricots, and cantaloupe into a blender and give it a spin.
2. Add the chilled water and stir gently. Mix well.
3. Pour the smoothie into two glasses, add the lime juice, and a pinch of Himalayan pink salt.
4. Stir well before drinking.

Raspberry, Chia, And Coconut Water Smoothie

Calories: 123/**Fat:** 6g

Carbohydrates: 18g/**Protein:** 5g

Prep Time: 5 minutes

Servings: 2

Ingredients

- ½ cup raspberries
- 2 tbsp. chia seeds
- 2 cup coconut water
- a handful of mint leaves

Instructions

1. Blend the raspberries and the mint leaves.

2. Add the coconut water and stir gently.

3. Pour it out into two glasses.

4. Add the chia seeds and stir well.

Gourd, Cucumber, And Lemon Smoothie

Calories: 114/**Fat:** 1g

Carbohydrates: 22g/**Protein:** 5g

Prep Time: 5 minutes

Servings: 2

Ingredients

- 1 cup bottle gourd/Lauki Juice (easily available on local market or amazon)
- 1 cup chopped cucumber
- ¼ cup chilled water

- 2 tbsp. lemon juice
- a pinch of Himalayan pink salt

Instructions

1. Toss the shredded bottle gourd and chopped cucumber into a blender and give it a spin.

2. Add the chilled water and lemon juice and stir well.

3. Pour the smoothie into two glasses.

4. Add a pinch of Himalayan pink salt and stir well before drinking.

Beetroot, Black Grape, And Mint Smoothie

Calories: 124/**Fat:** 3g

Carbohydrates: 18g/**Protein:** 3g

Prep Time: 8 minutes

Servings: 2

Ingredients

- ½ cup chopped beetroot
- 1 cup black grapes
- 2 tbsp. lime juice
- a handful of mint leaves
- a pinch of Himalayan pink salt

Instructions

1. Toss the chopped beetroot, black grapes, and mint leaves into a blender and blend well.

2. Pour the smoothie into two glasses.

3. Add lemon juice and a pinch of Himalayan pink salt and stir well.

Spinach, Strawberry, And Cinnamon Smoothie

Calories: 114/**Fat:** 1g

Carbohydrates: 22g/**Protein:** 5g

Prep Time: 5 minutes

Servings: 2

Ingredients

- 1 cup baby spinach
- ½ cup chopped strawberries
- ½ tsp. Ceylon cinnamon powder

Instructions

1. Blend the spinach and strawberries.

2. Pour the smoothie into two glasses.

3. Add the Ceylon cinnamon powder and stir well.

Banana, Almond, And Dark Chocolate Smoothie

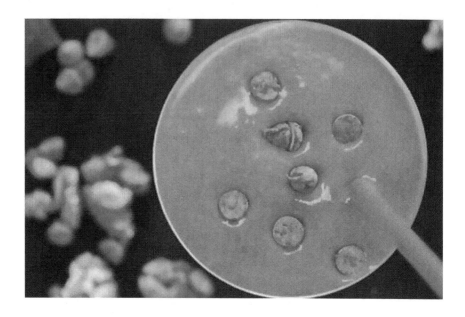

Calories: 140/**Fat:** 5g

Carbohydrates: 25g/**Protein:** 6g

Prep Time: 5 minutes

Servings: 2

Ingredients

- 1 cup sliced banana
- 8 almonds, soaked overnight

- 4 tablespoons grated dark chocolate, 80% cocoa
- ½ cup chilled low-fat milk

Instructions

1. Toss the sliced bananas, almonds, grated dark chocolate, and chilled milk into a blender and give it a spin.
2. Pour the smoothie into two glasses and relish.

Papaya, Lemon, And Cayenne Pepper Smoothie

Calories: 121/**Fat:** 6g

Carbohydrates: 20g/**Protein:** 4g

Prep Time: 5 minutes

Servings: 2

Ingredients

- 2 cup papaya
- 3 tbsp. lemon juice
- ½ tsp. cayenne pepper

Instructions

1. Blend the papaya.

2. Pour it out into two glasses.

3. Add lemon juice and cayenne pepper.

4. Stir well before drinking.

Pomegranate, Tangerine, And Ginger Smoothie

Calories: 114/**Fat:** 1g

Carbohydrates: 22g/**Protein:** 5g

Prep Time: 10 minutes

Servings: 2

Ingredients

- ½ cup pomegranate
- 1 cup tangerine
- 1 inch crushed ginger root
- a pinch of Himalayan pink salt

Instructions

1. Toss the pomegranate, tangerine, and ginger root into a blender and give it a spin.

2. Pour the smoothie into two glasses and add a pinch of Himalayan pink salt.

3. Stir well.

3. Green Smoothies

Cucumber Ginger Green Smoothie

Calories: 124/**Fat:** 2g

Carbohydrates: 15g/**Protein:** 4g

Prep Time: 10 minutes

Servings: 2

Ingredients

- 1 1/2 cup water
- 1 lemon, juiced
- 1/4 avocado, peeled and pitted
- 1 cup baby spinach
- 1/2 cup cucumber, peeled and seeds removed
- 2 dates or Medjool dates, pitted (available on amazon)
- 2 tbsp. hemp seeds

- 1/2 tsp. ground ginger
- 2 dashes fine sea salt to taste
- 1 cup ice cubes

Instructions

1. Add ingredients to high-speed blender in the order they are listed.
2. Begin blending on low and increase to highest speed.
3. Blend of high for approximately 35 seconds.

Peach Green Smoothie

Calories: 120/**Fat:** 3g

Carbohydrates: 20g/**Protein:** 4g

Prep Time: 10 minutes

Servings: 2

Ingredients

- ½ cup almond milk from a carton — you can also use water, coconut water, or coconut milk
- 1 cup baby spinach
- 1 medium ripe bananas, peeled, and frozen into chunks
- ¾ cup frozen peach chunks

- juice of half a lemon
- 1 tbsp. chia seeds

Instructions

1. Add all the ingredients to a blender and puree for about 30 seconds.
2. Taste to adjust flavor and serve immediately.

Peach Walnut Smoothie

Calories: 114/**Fat:** 1g

Carbohydrates: 22g/**Protein:** 5g

Prep Time: 5 minutes

Servings: 2

Ingredients

- 1 peach, sliced, pit removed, fresh or frozen
- 1/4 cup walnuts, chopped
- 1/4 tsp. cinnamon
- 1 tsp. coconut oil
- 1 cup spinach, packed

- 1/4 tsp. vanilla powder or extract (optional, skip this if you are using vanilla protein powder)
- 1 serving vanilla protein powder, optional
- 1/2 cup water
- 3 to 4 ice cubes

Instructions

1. Put all ingredients into a blender and blend until smooth.
2. Pour into your favorite glass and enjoy!

Fat-Burning Green Smoothie

Calories: 145/**Fat:** 4g

Carbohydrates: 25g/**Protein:** 6g

Prep Time: 5 minutes

Servings: 2

Ingredients

- 2 handfuls baby spinach
- 1 ripe banana
- 1 cup almond milk
- 1 cup frozen pineapple chunks

- 1/2 tsp. of ginger
- 1 tbsp. chia seeds

Instructions

1. Place all of the ingredients into a blender. Pulse until smooth.
2. If smoothie is too thick, add water. If too thin, add ice.
3. Serve and garnish with a sprinkle of chia seeds, optional.

Cucumber-Mint Smoothie

Calories: 114/**Fat:** 1g

Carbohydrates: 22g/**Protein:** 5g

Prep Time: 5 minutes

Servings: 2

Ingredients

- 1 cucumber, sliced (fresh or frozen)
- 1/4 cup-3/4 cup unsweetened vanilla almond milk (1/4 cup if using fresh cucumber, 3/4 cup if using frozen cucumber)

100

- 3 large mint leaves
- 1/2 tsp. pure stevia powder
- 1 cup ice

Instructions

1. Place all ingredients in the blender and blend until smooth. Enjoy!

Mango Matcha Green Smoothie

Calories: 170/**Fat:** 5g

Carbohydrates: 25g/**Protein:** 7g

Prep Time: 5 minutes

Servings: 2

Ingredients

- 1/2 avocado
- 1/2 tsp. matcha green tea
- 1/2 cup mango
- 1 cup baby greens,
- 1 cup almond milk
- stevia to taste

Instructions

1. Add everything but the avocado to a high speed blender and blend for a minute or two until you see that all the greens are well blended.

2. Then add your avocado and blend until nice and creamy.

3. If this is too creamy, add some more almond milk or water a little at a time.

4. You can add flax to this too if you want a little more fiber.

Green Spirulina Smoothie

Calories: 225/**Fat:** 10g

Carbohydrates: 36g Protein: 6g

Prep Time: 5 minutes

Servings: 2

Ingredients

For Smoothie:

- 1 medium ripe banana, peeled and frozen
- 1/2 cup sliced cucumber
- 3/4 - 1 cup light coconut milk
- 1 cup spinach or chopped kale

- 1 tsp. spirulina powder (you can buy it from amazon)
- 1 tbsp. hemp seed

For Serving, Optional:
- 1/4 cup frozen or fresh blueberries
- 1/4 cup granola

Instructions

1. To a blender, add frozen banana, cucumber, coconut milk, spinach, spirulina, and hemp seed (optional). Blend until creamy and smooth, scraping down sides as needed.

2. If too thick, thin with water or more coconut milk. If too thin, thicken with ice or more frozen banana. Taste and adjust flavor as needed, adding more banana for sweetness, cucumber for freshness, or greens or spirulina for green color.

3. Serve immediately as is or top with blueberries, granola, and more hemp seeds. Best when fresh, though leftovers will keep covered in the refrigerator up to 2 days or the freezer for 1 week. Thaw to enjoy from freezer.

Cold Buster Citrus Green Smoothie

Calories: 150/**Fat:** 5g

Carbohydrates: 20g/**Protein:** 4g

Prep Time: 5 minutes

Servings: 2

Ingredients

- 1 (5.3 – 6 oz.) container blood orange Greek yogurt
- 1 tbsp. lemon juice + ½ tsp. lemon zest
- 2 oranges, peeled
- ¼ tsp. turmeric powder
- 1 tsp. grated ginger

- 2 cup packed baby spinach
- ½ cup ice
- honey (optional)
- protein powder (optional)

Instructions

1. Add all the ingredients into a blender and process to desired consistency. Serve immediately.

Creamy Kiwi Smoothie

Calories: 153/**Fat:** 5g

Carbohydrates: 26g/**Protein:** 4g

Prep Time: 5 minutes

Servings: 2

Ingredients

- 1 1/2 oz. baby spinach
- 1 pear, chopped
- 2 kiwis, peeled

- 3 tbsp. cashews
- 1 cup water
- 1 cup ice

Instructions

1. Add all the ingredients into a blender and process to desired consistency. Serve immediately.

Chia Seed Smoothie

Calories: 153/**Fat:** 5g

Carbohydrates: 26g/**Protein:** 4g

Prep Time: 5 minutes

Servings: 2

Ingredients

- 2 cup spinach
- 1 cup water
- 2 oranges, peeled

- 1 cup pineapple
- 2 tbsp. chia seeds

Instructions

1. Blend spinach, water, and oranges together until smooth.
2. Add remaining ingredients and blend again.

Green Monster Smoothie

Calories: 153/**Fat:** 5g

Carbohydrates: 26g/**Protein:** 4g

Prep Time: 5 minutes

Servings: 2

Ingredients

- 3/4 cup plain Greek yogurt
- 1 scoop whey isolate protein powder
- 1/2 cup green grapes
- 1 kiwi, peeled
- 1 banana, peeled
- 1 green apple, cored

- 1/2 cup pineapple
- 1/2 cup kale, stems removed
- 6 ice cubes

Instructions

1. Combine all ingredients in a blender and blend until smooth.

Spicy Tropical Greens Delight

Calories: 148/**Fat:** 5g

Carbohydrates: 26g/**Protein:** 4g

Prep Time: 5 minutes

Servings: 2

Ingredients

- 1 cup frozen mango chunks

- 1 cup frozen pineapple chunks

- 1 1/2 unsweetened coconut water

- 1 cup leafy greens (baby spinach, kale, collard greens, etc.)

- 1/4 cup lime juice

- 1/4 tsp cayenne pepper (optional)

Instructions

1. Blend all ingredients together and enjoy.

Strawberry Spinach Green Smoothie

Calories: 163/**Fat:** 1g

Carbohydrates: 40g/**Protein:** 3g

Prep Time: 5 minutes

Servings: 2

Ingredients

- 1 1/2 very ripe bananas, peeled, diced and frozen
- 6 oz. fresh strawberries, hulled (about 9 medium)
- 2 mandarin oranges, peeled and halved
- 3 cup packed baby spinach

- 1 cup cold water
- 1 cup ice

Instructions

1. Add bananas, strawberries, oranges, spinach, water, and half of the ice to a blender.
2. Blend until combined then add remaining ice and blend until smoothie is well pureed. Serve immediately.

Vanilla-Mint Green Smoothie

Calories: 113/**Fat:** 1g

Carbohydrates: 20g/**Protein:** 3g

Prep Time: 5 minutes

Servings: 2

Ingredients

- 1/2 frozen banana
- 1 1/2 cup fresh spinach

- 10-15 fresh mint leaves
- 1/4 cup coconut milk

Instructions

1. Thoroughly blend until all ingredients are smooth. Serve immediately.

Tropical Green Smoothie

Calories: 429/**Fat:** 6g

Carbohydrates: 87g /**Protein:** 13g

Prep Time: 5 minutes

Servings: 2

Ingredients

- 1 to 2 cups frozen spinach
- 1 cup frozen pineapple chunks
- 1 cup frozen mango chunks
- 1 medium ripe banana, peeled
- 1 cup strawberries, blueberries, raspberries, or a favorite berry, optional

- 1 cup milk
- 1 tsp. vanilla extract
- sweetener, to taste

Instructions

1. All ingredients and amounts are to taste. Use seasonal fruits or vary the quantities of fruits, to taste. Use frozen fruit and prefer it to fresh because it keeps the smoothie cold, without adding ice which waters it down.

2. Place all ingredients in the canister of a blender and blend until smooth and creamy. Serve immediately. Pour extra portions into freezer-safe cups and freeze for up to one month, thawing before serving.

3. Optionally, consider adding a scoop of protein powder, dollop of yogurt for extra protein; add fat for staying power such as coconut oil, coconut butter, peanut butter, almond/cashew/sunflower seed/Cookie Butter. Blend with juice to increase the amount of Vitamin C. Add coconut flakes, nuts, seeds, dried fruits, or your favorite smoothie add-ins to either the blender canister before blending or garnish smoothie with them after blending.

Basil Cantaloupe Smoothie

Calories: 101/**Fat:** 1g

Carbohydrates: 21g/**Protein:** 5g

Prep Time: 5 minutes

Servings: 2

Ingredients

- 1 1/2 oz. baby spinach
- 4 oz. cantaloupe
- 1 pear, chopped
- 4 leaves basil
- 1 tsp. camu camu powder (easily available on amazon)
- 1 tbsp. pea protein

122

- 1 cup water
- 1 cup ice

Instructions

1. Place all ingredients into a blender.

2. Blend until smooth and no chunks remain.

3. Serve and enjoy.

Banana Blueberry Gooseberry Green Smoothie

Calories: 180/**Fat:** 3g

Carbohydrates: 30g/**Protein:** 4g

Prep Time: 5 minutes

Servings: 2

Ingredients

- 1 1/2 cup almond milk
- 1 big handful spinach
- 1 cup fresh blueberries
- 1/2 cup sliced banana (approximately 1 banana)
- 1/2 cup cape gooseberries

- 1 tbsp. flax seed
- 1 tbsp. almond butter
- 1 tbsp. raw agave

Instructions

1. Add the milk, spinach, banana, blueberries, flax seed, almond butter, and raw agave, in that order, to the blender.
2. Blend until smooth. Add ice to a large glass (optional) and pour the smoothie into glasses.

Kale Skin Tonic Green Smoothie

Calories: 130/**Fat:** 2g

Carbohydrates: 20g/**Protein:** 4g

Prep Time: 5 minutes

Servings: 2

Ingredients

- 1 cup of kale
- handful of parsley
- half of a medium size cucumber
- 2 celery sticks
- 3 Granny Smith apples
- juice of half a lemon

- juice of half a lime
- 1 cup of water

Instructions

1. In a high-speed blender, add the cup of water, kale, and parsley, then blend until smooth.
2. Next, add the celery and cucumber and blend again.
3. Lastly, add the apples and the juice of the lemon and lime and blend until smooth.
4. Serve and Enjoy!

Coconut Oil Detox Green Smoothie

Calories: 110/**Fat:** 1g

Carbohydrates: 18g/**Protein:** 3g

Prep Time: 5 minutes

Servings: 2

Ingredients

- 2 cup coconut milk or nut milk of choice
- 1 cup chopped organic spinach
- 1 cup chopped organic romaine lettuce or other salad greens
- 1/2-1 avocado, chopped
- 1 tbsp. raw, virgin, and unrefined coconut oil

- 1 tsp. spirulina powder
- 1 tsp. of lemon or lime juice
- 2-3 raw dates, pitted
- additional raw honey to taste (optional)
- pinch of sea salt

Instructions

1. Blend all ingredients and serve immediately.

Broccoli Detox Smoothie

Calories: 190/**Fat:** 2g

Carbohydrates: 43g/**Protein:** 4g

Prep Time: 5 minutes

Servings: 1

Ingredients

- 3/4 cup broccoli florets, chopped
- 1 banana
- 1/2 cup pineapple cut in chunks
- 1/2 cup almond milk
- 1/2 tsp. flax seeds, optional

Instructions

1. Place all the ingredients in your blender and blend!
2. Pour in glass and decorate with some frozen strawberries if you like.

Main Ingredients Used and its Benefits

Banana: They blend beautifully into nearly any recipe and provide a sweetness and creaminess that compliments the savory flavor of greens. Plus, they're full of potassium, which wards against cramps and helps lower blood pressure.

Collard Greens: It helps to keep bones strong and healthy — a plus for a lot of women. Many people think taking a calcium supplement is the only way to keep their bones strong, but a few cups of collard greens a week is a huge help!

Chia Seeds: Chia seeds are among the healthiest foods in the world. These tiny seeds are loaded with nutrients proven to energize, satiate, and even aid in weight loss. Plus, chia seeds have virtually zero taste, which makes them an ideal addition to almost any smoothie.

Apricot: Apricots are a good source of catechins, a family of flavonoid phytonutrients. These small fruits contain four to five grams of the anti-inflammatory catechins, as well as vitamins A and C.

Apple cider vinegar: One of most helpful alternative medicines out there, doing everything from controlling blood sugar spikes to aiding digestion and weight loss to even helping cure UTIs and sinus issues.

Avocados: Not only do they provide your body with the good kind of fat (fat that keeps your metabolism revved up), they also tell your body's fat storage hormones to turn off, making it more difficult for fat cells to actually build up.

Cinnamon: While cinnamon doesn't exactly boost your metabolism by itself, it does help fat cells respond better to insulin, which aids in sugar being processed more efficiently in your body. An efficient sugar process means more energy, less stored fat!

Yellow Peppers, Pineapple, Oranges: These are the foods which are high in Vitamin C. Vitamin C is crucial to the production of carnitine, a molecule that helps your muscles get their energy from fat. A study was even published in the *Journal of Nutrition* that found "people with higher levels of C in their blood had lower BMIs and less body fat."

Whey Protein: High-quality whey protein is a pretty important component when you're trying to lose weight. When you're shedding fat via a diet or exercise regime, you want to make sure you're not shedding muscle along with it and supplementing your diet with a smoothie full of whey (or another high-quality protein) keeps your muscles full and your metabolism working at full speed.

Zucchini: Zucchini has a good amount of lutein and zeaxanthin, phytonutrients that promote healthy eyesight. If you want a side dish that has a lot of health benefits but not a lot of calories, then zucchini is for you. Coming in at only 21 calories a cup, you can add some spices, salt and pepper, and saute yourself a satisfying, low-calorie side.

Carrots: With an abundance of vitamins A, C, K, E, beta-carotene, fiber, potassium, folate, manganese, and antioxidants, carrots have never been more appealing!

Asparagus: This green veggie's Folate content is known to be a mood booster and stress-reducer; plus, according to the Environmental Working Group, it is among the vegetables least likely to contain pesticide residue, providing yet another reason why you can eat it happily!

Grapefruit: Grapefruit's dense peel helps keep pesticides away from the juicy fruit. This is another reason why you can indulge on this low-sugar, vitamin C filled treat without an ounce of guilt.

Mango: This rich and creamy fruit is another one that can be eaten without worry thanks to its thick peel that protects its insides from toxic chemicals.

Mushrooms: Mushrooms are some of the least pesticide-ridden vegetables. They're also rich in B vitamins, magnesium, phosphorous, potassium, selenium, and fiber.

Papayas: This exotic fruit is rich in vitamins A, B, E, and K, as well as vital antioxidants.

Cantaloupe: Cantaloupes have thick outer skins; therefore, their juicy insides are protected from harmful pesticides.

Matcha: Matcha is also full of catechins and antioxidants that have been shown to help fight against, and possibly even prevent, cancer.

Turmeric: Turmeric has been used for centuries as a flavoring and in folk medicine, but it's one of the few superfoods that actually has the science to back up some of its long-touted healing properties.

Ginger: It will help that nauseous feeling go away. It soothes sore muscles, improves circulation, and could even ward off certain cancers.

Beets: They help your blood and brain fight degenerative diseases and also improve your performance at the gym.

Strawberries: A fat free and low calorie food, strawberries are full of fiber. They're also full of polyphenols, antioxidants that have been specifically categorized as cancer fighters (red wine and green tea have them too). Eight regular-sized strawberries will give you almost a full day's worth of vitamin C, and eating strawberries may also help in removing surface stains and plaque from teeth.

Conclusion

CONGRATULATIONS! On completing our book on 60 Delicious smoothies Recipes for Weight Loss' that will help you in improve your health and rapid weight loss! I hope you enjoyed this Green Smoothie Detox for Weight Loss!

This proven program will help you melt up to 15 lbs. of fat in just 10 days. And that's not all! You will also benefit from a huge array of other incredible health and beauty improvements.